REVISED EDITION

VIOLIN PIECES

THE WHOLE WORLD PLAYS

Selected and Edited by
ALBERT E. WIER
Editor of The "Whole World" Music Series

Copyright 1916 Embassy Music Corporation
33 West 60th Street, New York 10023

International Standard Book Number: 0-8256-1001-X

Distributed throughout the world by Music Sales Corporation:

33 West 60th Street, New York 10023
78 Newman Street, London W1P 3LA
4-26-22 Jingumae, Shibuya-ku, Tokyo 150
27 Clarendon Street, Artarmon, Sydney NSW
Kölner Strasse 199, 5000 Cologne 90

ALPHABETICAL CONTENTS

		VIOLIN	PIANO

To the Violinist

"VIOLIN Pieces The Whole World Plays" is designed to be the largest and most complete collection of standard violin masterpieces in the world. In this new, revised edition, several compositions are added which have become popular since the volume's first appearance more than ten years ago, so that practically every great composer, from Bach to Tschaikowsky, is now represented by a notably worthy composition. Lovers of this instrument will also be interested to note that the selections are not confined to those of any particular character. There is an almost equal choice of classic, of modern and of light violin compositions, and in this respect the book is not only unique, but indispensable as well to the amateur performer or the student.

THE EDITOR

Adagio

(From "Moonlight" Sonata)

L. VAN BEETHOVEN

"Minute" Waltz

FR. CHOPIN. Op. 64. Nº 1

Molto vivace
risoluto

Träumerei

R. SCHUMANN, Op. 15, Nº 7

Aria
(Caro mio ben)

G. GIORDANI

Nachtstück

R. SCHUMANN, Op. 23, № 4

18

Tempo I

L' Abeille
(The Bee)

FRANÇOIS SCHUBERT

20

Cradle Song

Andantino con molto espressione

M. HAUSER, Op. 11

23

Gavotte

F. J. GOSSEC

Minuet in G

L. VAN BEETHOVEN

Allegretto

TRIO

mf

bouncing stroke

mf

f

Minuet D.C.

Minuet D.C.

Loure

J. S. BACH

Allegro moderato

D.C. al Fine

Andante

C. W. GLUCK

Serenade

JOSEPH HAYDN

Andante cantabile

Air
(For the G-String)

J. S. BACH

Lento e molto espressivo

Nocturne

FR. CHOPIN, Op. 9, № 2

Melody in F

A. RUBINSTEIN

Spring Song
(Song Without Words No. 30)

F. MENDELSSOHN

Allegretto grazioso

47

Moment Musical

FR. SCHUBERT, Op. 94

Allegro moderato

Romance

A. RUBINSTEIN, Op. 44

Largo

G. F. HANDEL

Serenade
(Ständchen)

Fr. SCHUBERT

Andante con moto

Bourrée

G. F. HANDEL

Allegretto

Consolation

FR. LISZT

Mazurka

FR. CHOPIN. Op.7 № 1

Air
(Pur dicesti)

ANTONIO LOTTI

Minuet
(From Divertimento Nº17)

W. A. MOZART

Ave Maria
(Meditation)

BACH - GOUNOD

74

Fine

Andante
(From Violin Concerto)

RICHARD STRAUSS, Op. 8

Rêverie

CLAUDE DEBUSSY

An den Frühling
(To Spring)

EDWARD GRIEG

Tempo I

Chanson Triste

P. TSCHAIKOWSKY

Allegro non troppo

Poupée Valsante
(Waltzing Doll)

EDWARD POLDINI

Le Cygne

(The Swan)

C. SAINT- SAËNS

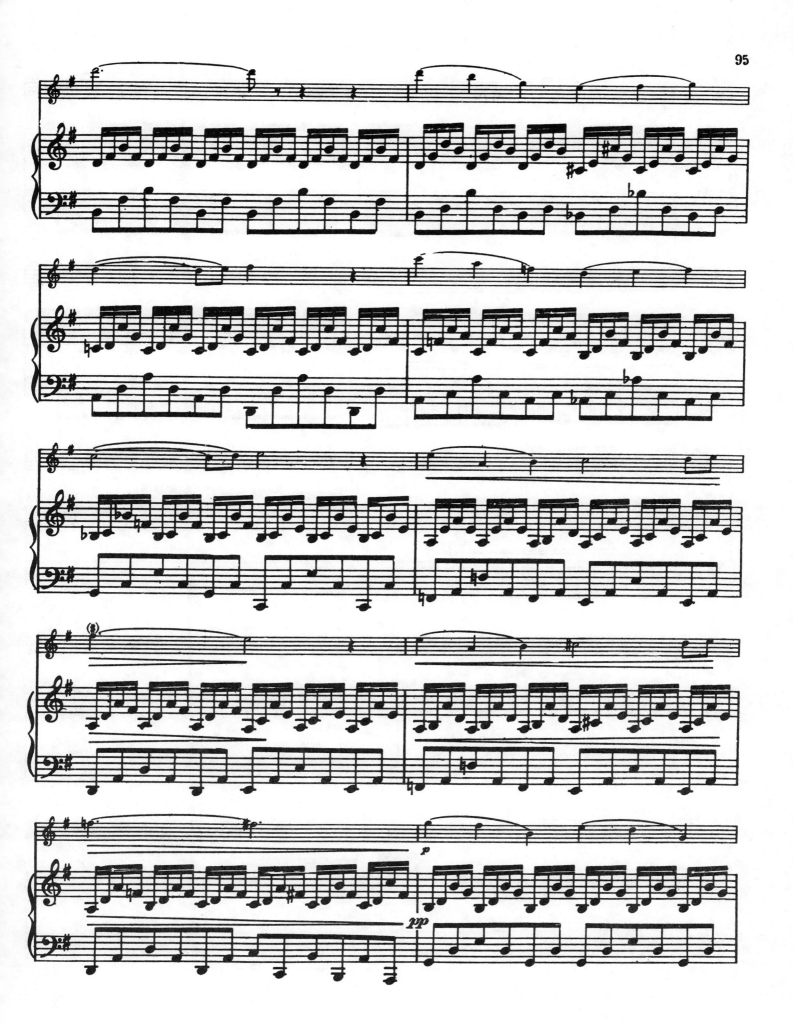

Anitra's Dance
(Peer Gynt)

EDWARD GRIEG

Tempo di Mazurka

Spanish Dance

M. MOSZKOWSKI. Op. 12, № 1

Allegro brioso

Souvenir

FRANZ DRDLA

Idyl

Allegretto quasi andantino

E. MACDOWELL, Op. 28, N° 1

Kujawiak
(Second Mazurka)

HENRI WIENIAWSKI

Tempo di Mazurka

112

Sérénade

G. PIERNÉ

Norwegian Dance

EDWARD GRIEG

Allegretto tranquillo e grazioso

Tempo I

Élégie
Mélodie

JULES MASSENET

Lento espressivo

Scarf Dance

CÉCILE CHAMINADE

Berceuse

EDWARD GRIEG

Con moto

Chant Sans Paroles
(Song Without Words)

P. TSCHAIKOWSKY

Allegretto grazioso e cantabile

Cavatina

JOACHIM RAFF

Salut d'Amour
(Love's Greeting)

EDWARD ELGAR

134

Minuet L'Antique

I. J. PADEREWSKI

CODA
Vivo

Polish Dance

X. SCHARWENKA. Op. 3, № 1

Con fuoco

Serenade

FRANZ DRDLA

147

Traum der Sennerin

(The Alp-Maid's Dream)

A. LABITZKY

151

Tempo Primo

152

Hungarian Dance No 5

JOHANNES BRAHMS

156 Vivace

Allegro

157

Humoreske

ANTON DVOŘÁK, Op. 101, Nº 7

Poco lento grazioso

Aragonaise

Azzez animé et trèz brillant

JULES MASSENET

Serenata

M. MOSZKOWSKI, Op. 15

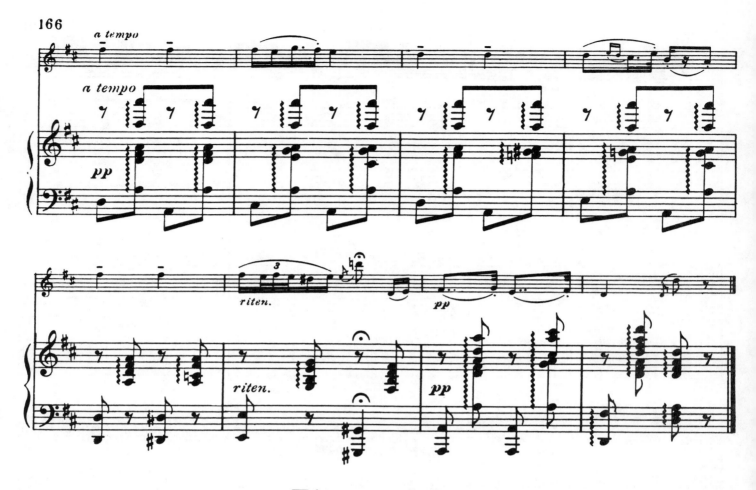

Flower Song
(Blumenlied)

GUSTAV LANGE

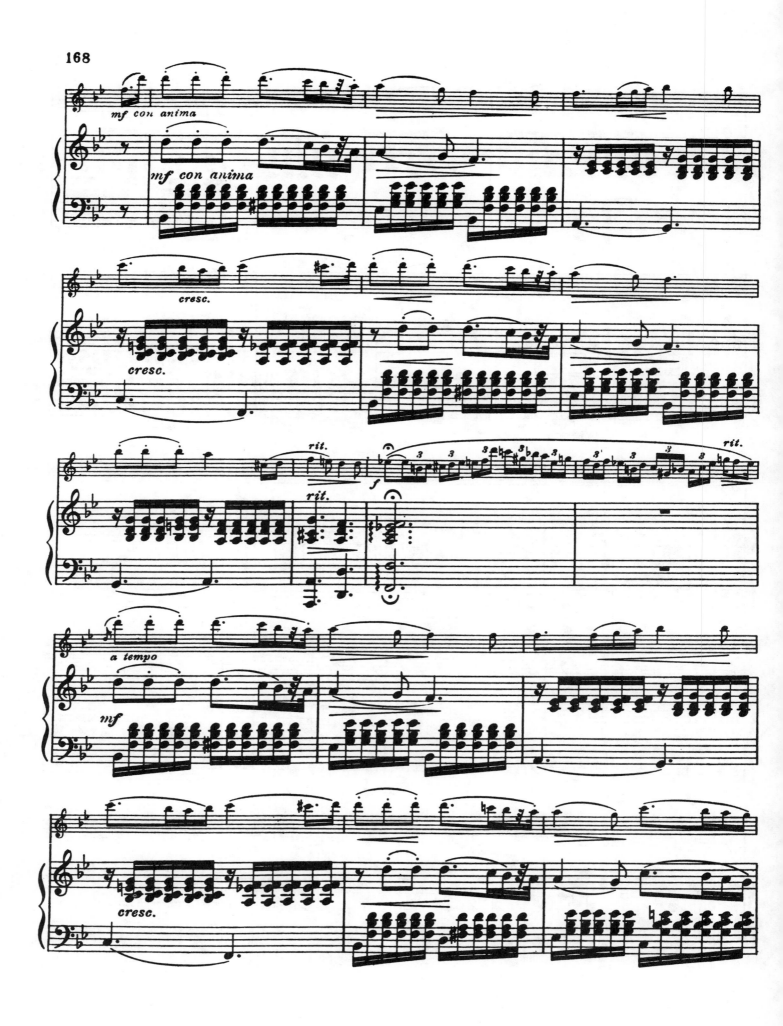

Berceuse

(From "Jocelyn")

BENJAMIN GODARD

Longing For Home
(Heimweh)

A. JUNGMANN

174

Valsette

Allegro

FÉLIX BOROWSKI

Tempo di Valse

Tempo Primo

Thine Own
(Dein Eigen)

GUSTAV LANGE

Andante espressivo

La Zingana

(Hungarian Mazurka)

CARL BOHM

Andante religioso

FRANCIS THOMÉ

Largamente

Tempo I

Simple Aveu

FRANCIS THOMÉ

Orientale

(From "The Kaleidescope")

CÈSAR CUI. Op. 50

Allegretto

Angel's Serenade
(La Serenata)

G. BRAGA

mf affrettando

poco più animato

cresc.

Tempo I.

The Rain
(Perpetuum Mobile)

CARL BOHM

Allegretto

Special Note - As originally written, the violin part of this composition is played in sixteenth notes, but a very pretty effect is gained by doubling the sixteenths.

Pizzicato

(From "Sylvia" Ballet)

L. DELIBES

Un poco più anima